Praise in

Poetry

Copyright © 2000
Barbara E. Rowan
browan@telusplanet.net

ISBN 0-9685056-2-7

Published by C. REALITY PUBLISHERS
Morinville, Alberta
c_realitypublishers@canada.com

Typesetting by Patrick Glenn,
Present Yourself Graphics, Edmonton, Alberta
pglenn@writeme.com

Printed in Canada by ART DESIGN PRINTING INC.
Edmonton, Alberta

Canadian Cataloguing in publication Data

Rowan, Barbara E., 1941-
Praise in poetry

1. Christian poetry, Canadian (English) 1. Title.*
PS8585.O8932P72 2000   C811'.6   C00-910862-9 PR9199.3.R633P72 2000

Contents

Foreword:

In each heart there is a hunger for a relationship with our Creator God.

A yearning to receive the gift of eternal life paid for on the Cross of Jesus Christ.

A longing for the companionship and empowerment of being indwelt by the Holy Spirit of God.

****

God's Word tells us in Romans, chapter 10 verse 9, "If you confess with your mouth the Lord Jesus, {speak the words out loud} and shall believe in your heart that God has raised Him from the dead, you shall be saved."

Precious one, Jesus loves you. Believe, confess to Him your sins, and ask Him to be Lord of your life. You will rejoice for all eternity over your decision!

Amen

Scripture quotations are taken from the Holy Bible, New King James Version.

Praise in Poetry

Dedications

I give thanks to our precious Holy Spirit
for flowing through me in praise.

"Bless the Lord, O my soul;
And all that is within me, bless His Holy name."
Psalm 103:1

I dedicate this book to the memory of Iva
McCrimmon, the Gramma who gave me the
best gift a Gramma can.
She taught me through Scripture verses, songs
and her love, that "Jesus loves me."

I thank God for my parents, Roy and Eileen
Armstrong; they have been faithful to me all
of my life.
I love you, Dad and Mom!

"The just man walks in his integrity: his children
are blessed after him."
Proverbs 20:7

To my beloved husband Chris, thank you.
To our children, Roxanne, Rick, Roy and
Rhonda, this praise in poetry is a part of the
generational blessing God has poured out on
this family, so evident in the poem, "The
Lord Will Provide" written by your Great,
Great-grandmother Caroline that is included
on page 40 of this book.

To my family and friends who have stood
with me in prayer and giving to see this
praise in print;

"I thank my God upon every
remembrance of you."
Philippians 1:3

To each one who reads the words on these
pages, may the Holy Spirit of our living God
lead you into a time of intimacy with our
Lord and Savior, Jesus Christ. Amen!

To God be the glory!

Praise in Poetry

Entering Into Your Presence!

I forgive those who hurt me, as You forgive me
I submit my life to You, Your servant I'll be.

Holy Spirit, overshadow my self- centered ways,
Anoint me and teach me to offer up praise!

I enter Your presence, through Your Blood at the Cross,
You rescued me Jesus, but oh what a cost!

My praise is the offering laid at Your feet,
Oh God, You are worthy, Your love is so sweet.

Dear God, how I love You, I rest in this place,
The warmth of Your Spirit helps me seek Your face.

Hallelujah!

"My heart is overflowing with a good theme;
I recite my composition concerning the King;
My tongue is the pen of a ready writer."
Psalm 45:1

Sweet Communion

Oh Lord, in sincere reverence this table I have spread
A menu of remembrance, the glass of wine, the bread.
The eve of Your betrayal, You taught us to partake
In emblems of the sacrifice, You would gladly make.

You offered thanks to God above,
then broke the loaf apart
To discern Your broken body does surely break my heart.
I remember now the price You paid,
in torture, grief and pain
You paid a ransom for me, my eternal love to gain.

The cup came next, a token of the spilling of Your Blood
Sealing a new covenant, a bond of priceless love.
We eat this bread and drink this cup,
as long as we draw breath
The price of our redemption
was our precious Savior's death.

Oh Jesus, how I love You, Your gift I do receive
The work You did on Calvary has taught me to believe.
Joy rises up within me - sweet praises fill this room
Jesus You're here with me, I see an empty tomb!

Hallelujah, Jesus Is Alive!

"And He took the bread, gave thanks and broke it, and gave it to
them , saying, 'This is My body which is given for you; do this in
remembrance of Me.' Likewise He also took the cup after supper
saying, 'This cup is the new covenant in My blood, which is shed
for you."

Amen

Luke 22: 19, 20

God's Beloved!

Behold God's Beloved,
Chosen to give
His life for a ransom that
others may live.
Behold God's Beloved,
Beloved of all,
Of us who have answered
salvation's call!

Behold God's Beloved,
my brother, my friend!
Through Him I found "Abba"
my joy does not end.

Behold God's Beloved,
beloved of all
of us who have answered
salvation's call!

Hallelujah!

*"For you did not receive the spirit of bondage
again to fear, but you received the Spirit of adoption
by whom we cry out, Abba, Father."*
Romans 8:15

Precious Blood!

Dear Jesus:

*We kneel as Your servants at the foot of Your Cross
Our eyes travel upward, as You pay the cost.*

*Your feet are before us, impaled and in pain
Your Blood courses downward, our freedom to gain.*

*Your body so ravaged, so tortured and torn,
the price You paid, Jesus, as our sins were borne.*

*Precious Blood drips upon us, so warm and so red,
through Your eyes of compassion, great tears are shed.*

*Oh Lord, we are washed in this cleansing flow,
our sins are forgiven, that we do know.*

*The stripes You endured that bruised and cut deep,
paid for the healing Your servants will keep.*

*You redeemed us Sweet Jesus, and now we survive
to rejoice in Your victory, thank God You're alive!*

*"But He was wounded for our transgressions,
He was bruised for our iniquities;
And by His stripes we are healed."*
Isaiah 53:5

Praise in Poetry

The New Bud!

Dear Jesus:

Sometimes my life seems anchored in the
things my senses know
The light of day, the dark of night, the
feel of warmth or cold.
By act of will, I lift my eyes above
this earthly place,
my spirit opens like a bud, I begin
to seek Your face.

Oh God, You're always there for me, You
love me through and through.
Forgive my time away, Dear Lord, please
hold me close to You.
Your peace now rests upon me, joy rises
up within,
I commit my life to serve You; help me
stay free from sin.

" As God has said:
I will dwell in them
And walk among them.
I will be their God,
And they shall be My people."
2 Corinthians 6:16

Praise!

Praise to You, my Jesus!
Praise to You, my Love!
You pour Your Spirit on me,
like a river from above.

O Living Water pour on through,
a flood of glistening rain.
I submit my very life to You,
please fill me up again!

Send tongues of spiritual fire,
great laser beams of light.
Do Your refining work in me,
Fresh fire make me right!
That I may grow in love for You,
praise pouring from my heart.
A vessel fully serving You,
a harvester, doing my part.

Amen!

*"When the Day of Pentecost had fully come, they were all with
one accord in one place. And suddenly there came a sound from
heaven, as of a mighty wind, and it filled the whole house where
they were sitting. Then there appeared to them divided tongues,
as of fire, and one sat on each one of them. And they were all
filled with the Holy Spirit and began to speak with other tongues,
as the Spirit gave them utterance."*
Acts 2: 1-4

Praise in Poetry

Halleluia, Jesus!

Praise and honor and glory to You,
Forgive me Lord, You see me through.

Washed in sacrificial Blood,
Your "Living Water" is a flood.
The redeeming, ever running stream,
Has freed me from the wicked scheme.

I claim prophetic destiny,
That as You tarry we will see
Your mighty harvest gathered in,
People turning from their sin.

This new Millennium will begin
With Revival Fire roaring in!

Amen

"Create in me a clean heart, O God
And renew a steadfast spirit within me.
Do not cast me away from Your presence,
and do not take Your Holy Spirit from me."
Psalm 51:10,11

The Road To Emmaus

Dear Jesus:
Two of Yours' were walking,
to Emmaus down the road.
Their shoulders slumped, their faces sad,
they carried such a load.
You came upon them from behind,
and asked them what was wrong
Their eyes were set, they knew You not,
but Cleopas spoke up strong.

"You must be a stranger here,
or surely You would know
They've crucified Jesus the Nazarene,
we truly loved Him so.
Our chief priests and our rulers
caused Him to be condemned
We had faith He was the One
to deliver sons of men.

Now it is the third day
since these dark deeds were done,
Some went to see His tomb
and found His body gone.
We were astonished
when the women testified
To a vision of Angels,
who said, He is alive!"

As You walked, You spoke to them
the things that God has willed.
Prophetic words that in this hour
had finally been fulfilled.
You came upon their village then,
they asked You to abide,
"Come in and sup with us,"
You graciously complied.

You took the bread, and blessed and broke,
then gave it unto them.
Their eyes were opened, they discerned,
they knew that You were Him.
They marveled as they made their way
back to Jerusalem.
"He spoke God's Word; did we not feel
the fire deep within?"

They found eleven gathered,
with friends in The Upper Room,
Cleopas and Simon
had news to break their gloom.
"It's really happened like He said,
the third day has arrived,
Our Master has been risen up,
JESUS IS ALIVE!"

Hallelujah.

Luke 24: 13-35

About Emmaus Road

Dearest Lord Jesus:
I ponder now the Scriptures,
from Luke twenty - four.
Emmaus Road, a few short miles,
but really so much more.
My life stretches back behind me now,
I see the way I've come.
So many miles, the heavy load,
but now I'm coming home!

Just as their eyes were set from You,
I have walked that way.
I tried so hard in my own strength,
to make it all okay,
Tears streaming down,
eyes set on self, wallowing in sin.
So much time wasted; but then...
I let You in!

When I came to the end,
of health and strength and pride
I found You'd been there always,
walking by my side.
My eyes were opened, You took my load,
You healed my broken heart,
You sup with me, You comfort me,
You always do Your part.

Thank You Jesus!

Come Soon, Lord Jesus!

You warned us to watch with spiritual eyes,
be alert to the schemes that the enemy tries.

Oh come soon - Lord Jesus, come soon
Beloved Redeemer, come soon.

We'll be sober and moderate, without undo care,
that Your return, Precious Jesus, not be a snare.

Oh come soon Lord Jesus, come soon-
Beloved Redeemer, come soon.

We'll watch and we'll pray, Lord, till You are in sight,
then we'll welcome our Bridegroom, the Giver of Light!

Oh come soon Lord Jesus, come soon-
Beloved Redeemer, come soon.

Amen!

"Heaven and earth will pass away; but My words will by no means pass away.

But take heed to yourselves, lest your hearts be weighed down with carousing, drunkenness, and the cares of this life, and that Day come upon you unexpectedly.

For it will come as a snare on all those who dwell on the face of the whole earth.

Watch therefore, and pray always, that you may be counted worthy to escape all these things that shall come to pass, and to stand before the Son of Man."

Luke 21:33-36

Praise in Poetry

The Parable Of The Vineyard

A certain man of vision sowed,
His fertile ground
with cuttings of a vineyard,
and fenced it all around.

He dug in a sturdy winepress,
and built a tower high
then entrusted it to farmhands,
he'd be back by and by.

He journeyed to a far country, and
at harvest time he sent
a servant to the vineyard
to collect his yearly rent.

The farmhands caught and beat him
and sent him home unfilled,
the Owner then sent others, some they stoned,
and some they killed.

In one last hope to reach them
the Owner sent his best,
his much beloved son
would stand up to the test.

But now the farmhands schemed,
this is the Owner's heir,
We'll kill him for the vineyard,
and never have to share.

His beloved son they killed,
what can the Owner do?
He'll come destroy the farmhands,
and restore those who are true.

The Holy Scripture's given,
we can read there on our own,
"The Stone, that the builder's rejected,
is now the Cornerstone."

Lord, Your work is marvelous in our eyes!

Amen

Mark 12: 1-11

Creation's Plan
Pondering the Parable of the Vineyard

Lord, You had a vision,
Creation's plan now birthed!
A garden of such beauty,
You planted here on earth.
You created birds and creatures,
the shade trees standing high,
Then entrusted it to mankind,
You'll come back by and by.

The far country is Your Heaven,
and often You have sent,
Your Prophets here among us,
the evil to prevent.
But we Your sinful people,
rebellious and strong willed,
Beat and stoned and mocked them,
some we even killed!

So in Your tender mercy,
for this people that You love,
Your Beloved Son fulfilled Your plan
and came down from above.
But we were so hardhearted,
we still would not repent,
We mocked and beat and scourged Him,
and to Calvary He went.

Oh God, You have tried everything,
so now what can You do?
You'll come destroy the wicked
and save those who are true.
We've read Your Holy Bible,
Your Word is now our own,
Your Son we have accepted - He is our Cornerstone!

To our God be the Glory!

Luke 20: 9-17

"Jesus"

My heart swells

A rushing mighty force.

There is no end, Lord,

Your love runs through on course.

It fills me, Love pours from above

My heart swells to bursting,

Flowing with love.

For You, Lord, Precious Holy One.

Amen

*"Therefore let all the house of Israel know assuredly
that God has made this Jesus, whom you crucified,
both Lord and Christ."*
Acts 2:36

Heaven

Oh Jesus, You endeavored, the mystery to explain
a magnificent inheritance, prepared for us to claim.

"What if I walked in a stranger's field and found pure gold?
I'd sell all and buy that field, the treasure just to hold.

Or if I were a merchant, and found a lovely pearl?
I'd part with all, that I might buy that very special jewel.

Again if the Kingdom of Heaven was like a fishing net?
Drawn in full, a mighty haul, the biggest one yet.

The fishermen would choose the best, and throw the rest away.
Just as God's Angels will with us on that final day."

Oh Jesus, now I understand and pray that I may be,
Covered by Your precious Blood, so heaven I will see.

Amen

"Again, the kingdom of heaven is like treasure hidden in a field, which a man found and hid; and for joy over it he goes and sells all he has and buys that field.

Again, the kingdom of heaven is like a merchant seeking beautiful pearls: who, when he had found one pearl of great price, went and sold all that he had, and bought it.

Again the kingdom of heaven is like a dragnet, that was cast into the sea, and gathered some of every kind, which, when it was full, they drew to shore; and they sat down, and gathered the good into vessels, but cast the bad away. So it will be at the end of the age. The angels will come forth, separate the wicked from among the just, and cast them into the furnace of fire. There will be wailing and gnashing of teeth."

Matthew 13:44-50

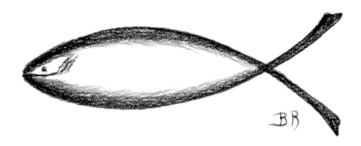

Behold The Son

Behold You come upon the clouds,
that each of us may see,
Our hearts will break within us as we
remember Calvary's tree.

Oh King of Kings, Lord of Lords, help
me to comprehend,
You are my Alpha and Omega, my
beginning and my end.

I praise You precious Jesus, I praise
Your Holy Name!
The first, the last, the always, You'll
ever be the same.

I love the way You love me,
I hold Your gentle hand,
Your presence is upon me,
Holy Spirit fill this land.

Amen

"Behold, He is coming with clouds;
and every eye shall see Him
and even they who pierced Him.
And all the tribes of the earth will mourn because of Him.
Even so, Amen.

'I am the Alpha and the Omega,
the beginning and the end,'
says the Lord who is, and who was, and who is to come,
the Almighty."

Revelation 1: 7&8

Sovereign God
Supreme in Majesty!
Thy will be done,
From sea to sea

Amen

Follow Me!

As Jesus went, two followed;
He asked them, "What seek ye?"
"Rabbi, where do You dwell?"
Jesus answered, "Come and see."
They came and saw and did abide,
just as with you and me.
We hear the call of our dear Lord,
as He says "Follow Me."

Andrew knew he'd found the truth,
and did what's right for all.
"Simon, we have found Messiah!"
It's the Great Commissions' call!
Jesus looked at Simon,
the call on his life well known,
"Your name is Simon, I'll call you Cephas,
for you will be a stone."

The next day as He traveled,
on His way to Galilee,
Jesus came to Philip, and invited,
"Follow Me!"
Then Philip met Nathaniel, and said
"We've found the One,
of whom the prophets preached,
Jesus the Nazarene, Joseph's Son."
"Oh Philip, out of Nazareth
can any good thing come?"

Jesus heard Nathaniel,
and proclaimed with a smile,
"Behold an Israelite indeed,
in whom there is no guile."

Nathaniel then questioned
"From whence knowest thou me?"
"Before Philip called, I saw you
under the fig tree."

Oh Precious Lord, we now say,
just like Nathaniel,
"Rabbi, You are the Son of God,
the King of Israel."
Just as You spoke to him,
You speak to us today
Then as we seek to know You...
You answer when we pray.

Amen!

John 1:37-50

Spiritual Light!

Shine on me Jesus, light up this face

Help me to grow in Your mercy and grace.

...

Shine through me Jesus, with Your pure clean light

That I may draw others from Satan's dark night.

...

The light that is shed from your glorious Word

Cuts through the darkness; a two-edged sword.

...

Oh thank You sweet Jesus, that You make a way

You paid with Your Blood what we could not pay.

"I can do all things through Christ who strengthens me."
Philippians 4:13

The Guest

The kitchen smelled its very best
the finest table laid
The home of Lazarus was blessed
with a special Guest today.

Martha cooked and worked so hard
did everything she could,
While Mary sat at Jesus' feet
to hear His every word.

Then a new smell filled the home
a fragrance rare and sweet
A precious ointment poured upon
our Savior's beautiful feet.

Oh may I choose the loving part
as Mary did that day
A sweet smell reaching upward, Lord
as I pause to pray!

Amen.

"There they made Him a supper; and Martha served, but Lazarus
was one of those who sat at the table with Him. Then took Mary
a pound of very costly oil of spikenard, anointed the feet of Jesus,
and wiped his feet with her hair. And the house was filled with
the fragrance of the oil."
John 12:2&3

The Lord Will Provide

Written by Caroline Melissa Bowen,
Great-grandmother of author. Written March 10, 1907.
Caroline was born May 17, 1848 and died June 12, 1908.

Tho trouble assail
And dangers affright
Though friends should all fail
And foes all unite,
Yet one thing secures us
Whatever betide
The Scriptures assure us
The Lord will provide.

The birds without barn
Or storehouse are fed
From them let us learn
To trust for our bread.
His saints, it is fitting
Shall not be denied.
So long as 'tis written
The Lord will provide.

His call we obey
Like Abram of old
Not knowing our way
But faith makes us bold.
And though we are strangers
We have a good guide.
And trust through all dangers
The Lord will provide.

We may, like the ships
In tempests be tossed
On perilous deeps
But cannot be lost.
Though Satan enrages
The wind and the tide.
The promise engages
The Lord will provide.

When Satan appears
To stop our own path
And fills us with fears
We triumph by faith.
He cannot take from us
Tho oft he has tried,
Our heart cheering promise
The Lord will provide.

He tells us we're weak
Our hope is in vain.
The good that we seek
We'll never obtain.
But when such suggestions
Our spirits have tried,
This answers all questions
The Lord will provide.

No strength of our own
Or goodness we claim
But since we have known
The Savior's great name.
In this our strong tower
For safety we hide.
The Lord is our power
The Lord will provide.

When life sinks a pace
And death is in view
This work of His grace
Shall comfort us through.
No fearing nor doubting
With Christ on our side
We hope to die shouting
The Lord will provide!

Praise in Poetry

Thy Will Be Done

God's will be done:
in my Nation
God's will be done:
in my life
God's will be done:
in my family
God's Word cut through
like a knife.

O God there is joy in submitting!
In trusting all to You
It's a peace I don't understand
A security that is new.

There's a song alive in my spirit
A flowing of love in my heart
Your purpose and plan clear before me
A future where I have a part.

Amen

Our Father in heaven,

Hallowed be Your name.

Your kingdom come

Your will be done

On earth as it is in heaven.

Give us this day our daily bread.

And forgive us our debts,

As we forgive our debtors.

And lead us not into temptation,

But deliver us from the evil one.

For Yours is the kingdom and

the power and the glory forever,

and ever.

Amen

Good Shepherd

A shepherd's heart is faithful,
he'll stand up for his flock
The sheep are his, he knows their worth,
he guards the way they walk.
But if they were another's sheep,
and he a hired hand,
he'd turn and flee from danger
when it stalked them in the land.

Lord, You are the good Shepherd,
Your love for us is true,
We know Your loving kindness,
and we are known of You.
Just as the Father knows You,
and You are part of God,
You came to give Your life for us,
You gladly shed Your Blood.

You willed to lay Your life down,
for the sheep within Your fold,
But more than that for lost ones,
spread out around the world.
That they shall recognize You
and know they hear Your voice,
We'll all be in one sheep fold,
and God's Son will be our choice.

For You are God's beloved Son,
and You set forth a plan,
That You would give Your life for us,
then take it up again.
No man could take Your life from You,
no man could make You stand,
The power to give, and the power to take,
is Yours by God's command.

Thank You Jesus!

John 10: 11-18

Praise in Poetry

Nicodemas

Dear Jesus:

The night was dark, the hour late,
when Nicodemas came
an important Pharisee,
he asked You to explain.
"Rabbi, we see You are a teacher
God has sent this hour
for man cannot do miracles,
without God's mighty power."

Lord, what man must do,
You told him clearly then
**"Truly, if you would see God,
you must be born again."**

*"Jesus answered and said to him,
Most assuredly, I say to you, unless one is
born again, he cannot see the kingdom of God."*
John 3:3

Praise in Poetry

My Life

All of my days my heart really knew
My reason for life, Lord, was to magnify You.
As a child, You were love, Lord, and laughter and play
A new baby sister, that You sent my way
The love of my parents, my brothers, our farm
The times we were spared from serious harm.

Then in my teen-years, I asked You into my heart,
I tried to obey you, I would do my part;
But I fell so short, Lord, I sinned against You
My sin was deep scarlet, oh what could I do?
I cried and I pleaded, oh please forgive me
Your Blood was shed paying - so I could be free.

Oh God, I am sorry, it took me so long
Stuck in my grief, Lord, I was so wrong.
The pain and the sorrow over my sin
Caused me to believe I could not come back in.

Thank You dear Jesus, I finally knew
It's not about me, Lord, it's all about You.
Your life You laid down, Your Blood You shed,
You paid my debt, Lord, before I ever said,
"Forgive me, I'm sorry, restore me to You."
The past is forgotten, I'm really brand new!

"Therefore if anyone is in Christ, he is a new creation;
old things have passed away; behold, all things have
become new."
2 Corinthians 5:17

Lost In Sin

I was lost, deep in sin, a body of death,
About to give up, and draw my last breath.

I lay on my bed, at the end of my strength,
To solve sin's destruction, I'd gone to great length.

Then God's Holy Spirit witnessed to me,
In the Presence of God, " Would I be free?"

My life's work a failure, I looked to the Son
And spoke from my heart, " Thy will be done."

Now I am well and equipped to give,
God's Word to my neighbor, that others may live.

Thank You Jesus!

"For God has not given us (me) a spirit of fear, but of power
and of love and of a sound mind."
2 Timothy 1:7

Personal note from the author...
God used this verse of Scripture, as I memorized it and repeated
it hundreds of times in prayer, to set me free from a spirit of
timidity. (He also let me know that He changed my mind!)

Halleluia

Submission

Dear Jesus:

To the heart of my innermost being
The very core of my life.
I open myself to You, Jesus
Your laser beams of light.

The darkness flees before You
The sin, the shame and the scars.
I repent of the sin Your truth shows me
At the foot of a wooden Cross.

I throw myself on Your mercy
The Blood You shed just for me,
I receive the gift of forgiveness
Your sacrifice sets me free!

Oh Lord, I long to thank You
To bless Your heart with my praise.
To live a life of obedience,
Your law, my joy all my days.

For now I am become fruitful
A vine pruned, healthy and strong.
Equipped and serving Your purpose
My life a worship song!

Singing a song of Your beauty,
Your power, might and love.
Angels joining the worship,
A flood of praise high above.

*"You prepare a table before me in the presence of my enemies;
You anoint my head with oil; My cup runs over."*
Psalm 23:5

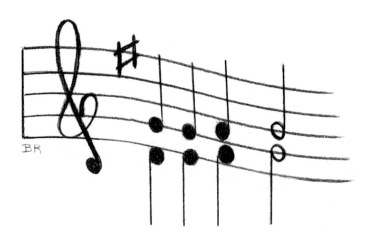

Praise in Poetry

Thanksgiving!

A song of praise is drifting through my mind today
I come into Your presence, with thankful heart to pray.

To lift Your name Jehovah, with a joyous shout
To love You and exalt You is what life is all about!

You showed me Lord, my sinful life and told me what to
do
I repented of my sin, and then I gave my heart to You.

The penalty for sin is death, but You had made a plan
Your life You'd give, Your Blood You'd shed to pay the
debt for man.

Oh Lord You have redeemed me, by Your precious Blood
Thank You God, You saved me, it's only You who could.

Now my life is Your life, for all eternity
Please make of me a vessel that fulfills its destiny.

*"Let us come before His presence with thanksgiving;
Let us shout joyfully to Him with psalms.*

*For the Lord is the great God,
And the great King above all gods."*
Psalm 95: 2 & 3

Turning From Sin

Let's turn from darkness
Let's turn from sin
Let's turn from destruction
Let's enter on in.

To Jesus, Redeemer
Healer of men
God's Son, Holy God,
Alive without end.

For Jesus is love,
He's all that is true
He suffered Calvary,
For me and for you.

There's a hope for the future
A way that is bright,
Intimate friendship with God
The Giver of Light.

"Your word is a lamp unto my feet and a light unto my path."
Psalm 119:105

Lord, Heal Our Land!

Oh Lord, I am Yours, bought with Your Blood
forgiven and ransomed, filled with Your love.
I thank You, my Jesus, for making a way
Now take me and use me for others I pray.

I stand in the gap for this Nation of ours
we began with such promise of blessing and power.
Our people grew cold, hardhearted and stiff,
Eyes seeing, but blind; ears hearing, but deaf.

You said if Your people, called by Your Name
would call for Your mercy, You'd hear us again.
I bow humbly before You, repenting of sin
I seek Your face early; may I enter in?

Your Throne Room before me, I boldly draw near
and stand on Your promise; You really do hear
the cries of Your people, in Satan's cruel hand.
Oh praise You dear Jesus, You will heal our Land!

━━━━━━━

" If My people, which are called by My name, shall humble
themselves, and pray, and seek My face, and turn from their wicked
ways; then will I hear from heaven, and will forgive their sin, and
heal their land."
2 Chronicles 7:14

Prayer For Peace, Oh Jerusalem

Dear Jesus:

Rejoicing, I soar in my spirit
To the lovely Temple of God
Jerusalem, city of worship
Built on Israels' sod.

As one of the peoples of Canada
For the sake of my family and friends
For the sake of God's Holy Temple,
Jerusalem prayer never ends.

Now I see the natural
A city on foreign ground.
The prophetic hour is coming when
A New Jerusalem will be found.

Magnificent in her splendor,
Alight with the Presence of God!
Descending down from the Heavens
Fulfilling God's prophetic Word.

So now I stand as a watchman
And Israel's boundaries defend.
Peace be upon that Nation;
Canada is my country, Jerusalem is my friend!

"Pray for the peace of Jerusalem:
May they prosper who love you.
Peace be within your walls,
Prosperity within your palaces."
Psalm 122: 6 & 7

Almighty God, Our King

Holy, living, reigning God, magnificent ruler supreme
Variety, color and symmetry declare Your designer theme.
Your power is displayed above in the beauty of the sky
Your care for us so evident, though we often wonder why.

The fragrance of the flowers, the shelter of the trees
The majesty I see in You sets my heart at ease.
Oh God, You are so loving I really can't describe
Your will to rescue all of us, from every tongue and tribe.

Oh pour out Holy Spirit,
on every living thing
That we may love and reverence
our precious God and King!

Pour out Holy Spirit, pour out!

"Lift up your heads, O you gates!
Lift up, you everlasting doors!
And the King of glory shall come in.
Who is this King of glory?
The Lord of hosts,
He is the King of glory."
Psalm 24:9, 10

Psalm Of Praise

I'll be Your vessel of praise, Lord
For You are my praiseworthy God.

I'll sing Your praise all my days, Lord
For You are my praiseworthy God.

I'll praise You in the morning
I'll praise You through the day,
In my sleep Your praise runs through me
As my spirit's moved to pray.

Halleluia, I will praise You
Halleluia all my days,
A life filled with thanksgiving
A vessel made for praise!

Amen

"Rejoice in the Lord, O you righteous!
For praise from the upright is beautiful.
Praise the Lord with the harp;
Make melody to Him with an instrument of ten strings.
Sing to Him a new song;
Play skillfully with a shout of joy."
Psalm 33:1-3

Creation

Mountains majestic
Valleys serene
The spruce and the poplar,
Shades of green.

Calling of birds
The beauty of flight.
Stars light the heavens;
A spectacular sight.

Oh Jesus, beloved
My God and my friend,
I see You in everything
Creator of men.

Thank You Jesus

"The Lord God planted a garden eastward in Eden, and there He put the man whom He had formed. And out of the ground the Lord God made every tree grow that is pleasant to the sight and good for food. The tree of life was also in the garden, and the tree of the knowledge of good and evil."
Genesis 2: 8 & 9

Precious Holy Spirit

Oh Holy Spirit, You are pouring
Living Water through my soul.

My spirit opens up in joy,
In love and strength made whole.

Fill me, fill me Jesus,
Wash the corners of my life.

In You there is no shadow,
In You there is just Light.

Pour that Light on through me,
A fire in my bones.

So I must share the Good News,
Of how Your Blood atones!

Amen

"How beautiful are the feet of those who preach the gospel of
peace. Who bring glad tidings of good things!"
Romans 10:15b

Resurrection Faith!

The ruler of the synagogue
had wealth and fame and power,
but status was as nothing
as he faced his crisis hour.
With broken heart and tear - filled eyes,
he fell at the Master's feet.
"My little daughter's dying, please come;"
he did entreat.

The Master followed after,
and then a servant said,
"Why trouble thou the Master?
Your little daughter's dead."
The father's footsteps faltered,
his heart began to grieve.
Then Jesus said with matchless love,
"Don't be afraid; only believe."

The man in faith then followed,
the crowd refused to wait,
when they reached the ruler's home,
they were stopped at the gate.
Lord, You asked the mourners;
"Why do you wail and weep?
The daughter is not dead at all,
but in a peaceful sleep."

The crowd began to laugh and scorn;
our Savior bid them, "Out!"
Just as in us, faith cannot work
in unbelief and doubt.
Lord, You drew the parents in
and took the little hand,
You spoke "Talitha Cumi"
and straightway the child did stand.

Dear Lord, You haven't changed at all,
You hear us when we pray,
Just as You healed this precious child,
You're healing us today!

Amen!

Mark 6: 35-42

Praise be to God

Lord, I give You glory, Your presence fills my life
Your grace enables me to stand through many kinds of strife.

Lord, that You could love me, could care so much for me
You must see something in me, that I could never see.

That in my very spirit, in my innermost heart,
You poured Your Holy Spirit, we never more shall part.

Oh Awesome God, so Holy, Omnipotent, Supreme,
to worship You completely is my sweetest dream.

That I may be a joy to You, a sweet smell rising up,
with gentle, useful hands, and thankful, loving heart.

Father God, You welcome me, Your arms receive me now
to rest in You, and live in You, is my solemn vow.

Amen

Earth Tones

May I tell a story of the color of our skin?
We think it caused division, but really, Satan entered in.
Division's never color, division's always sin.

Remember back in Genesis when God created man?
He made man of the dust that covered that good land.
So when we look at color, the shades of me and you
We see that we just represent our earth's natural hue.

There's white in stone and ice and snow,
and everywhere you go,
There's black in coal and minerals
And fertile living loam.

BR

Raw umber holds the tones of brown
The lake shores and the sand.
Burnt sienna, rock of red is
Often seen in man.

Then the yellow ochre, a
brownish yellow tone,
A shade of brown, a hint of sun
The Orient's alone.

So how can we but thank our God.
Our Maker whom we trust?
He made us represent the earth,
From which He created us.

Thanks be to God.

"The earth is the Lord's, and all its fullness,
The world and all that dwell therein."
Psalm 24:1

A Yoke Of Pleasure!

Lord, I thank You for inviting me to enter into You,

For the labors of this daily life
seemed never to be through.

Long years were filled with trouble,
I tried my very best,

Then You came to live within my heart,
and filled my life with rest.

I took Your yoke upon me,
and began to learn of You,

I found You meek and loving,
Your Word forever true.

For the yoke You placed upon me,
I carried with such ease,

Your burden rests so lightly,
to obey You is to please!

Lord Jesus I love You!

" For My yoke is easy, and My burden is light."
Matthew 11:30

Praise in Poetry

Heart Stayed on Jesus!

You teach us Lord,

to ponder what is pure and just and true.

Love, honor and virtue, the attributes of You!

To think on things of good report;

That are worthy of our praise.

It's You, dear precious Holy God, The Ancient of Days!

"Finally, brethren, whatever things are true, whatever things are honest, whatever things are just, whatever things are pure, whatever things are lovely, whatever things are of good report; if there is any virtue, and if there is anything praiseworthy — meditate on these things.

The things, which you learned and received, and heard and saw in me, these do, and the God of peace will be with you."
Philippians 4: 8&9

Stand!

And having done all to stand, stand.

Lord, it's Your Word for this hour,
When around me all looks gray.
I'll stand in the name of Jesus,
In faith for a bright new day.

Oh Lord, equip me with courage,
I stir up the embers of faith.
I'll not allow man to discourage.
On the course laid before me, I'll stay.

"Therefore take up the whole armor of God, that you may be able to withstand the evil day, and having done all, to stand. Stand therefore, having girded your waist with truth, having put on the breastplate of righteousness, and having shod your feet with the preparation of the gospel of peace; above all, taking the shield of faith with which you will be able to quench all the darts of the wicked one. And take the sword of the Spirit, which is the Word of God."

Ephesians 6:13-17

BR

Our Place

This place is so special, so Your's and so mine,

I enter Your presence, and exit from time.

My heart became heavy, laden with care,

the cares I cast to You, and enter with prayer.

Holy Spirit please fill me, descend like a dove

with the grace of our Jesus, His undying love.

Amen

"But seek first the kingdom of God and His righteousness, and all these things shall be added to you. Therefore do not worry about tomorrow, for tomorrow will worry about its own things. Sufficient for the day is its own trouble."
Matthew 6: 33 & 34

The Spirit Of The Living God!

John the Baptist heard the call of
God upon his life.

He served with faith, he paved the way, through
many miles of strife.

Then baptizing, he beheld the Spirit,
like a dove descend.

The Spirit of the Living God,
on the One who'd ransom men.

His face alight, heart filled with joy,
he introduced his Lord.

To those who stood around him,
"Behold the Lamb of God."

Thank you Jesus!

"And John bore witness saying, I saw the Spirit descending from heaven like a dove, and he remained upon Him. I did not know Him, but He who sent me to baptize with water said to me, 'Upon whom you see the Spirit descending , and remaining on Him, this is He who baptizes with the Holy Spirit. And I have seen and testified that He is the Son of God."

John 1: 32-34

The Glory

Dear Jesus

There is a lovely picture
painted in my heart
You stand there at the doorway
I raise my hand to knock.
But as I knock for entrance
preparing to walk through
I knock and You enfold me...
I've entered into You!

With loving arms around me
You take me through the door
into that Holy presence
God's Throne Room stands before.
Oh thank You for this vision
where at a door I stood
I've come into that Holy Place
through Your redeeming Blood.

Halleluia!

"Let us therefore come boldly to the throne of grace,
that we may obtain mercy and find grace in time of need."
Hebrews 4: 16

Praise in Poetry

You, Lord:

To worship You, to praise You,
To lift Your Name above
To stand for You and honor You,
And give You all my love.

That I may be a blessing,
Part of a fruitful vine,
Your Word upon my lips, Lord
Your light a living sign.

That others may approach You,
May reach out for Your hand
Your Presence flowing through me;
For healing in our Land.

Amen

"Abide in Me, and I in you. As the branch cannot
bear fruit of itself, unless it abides in the vine,
neither can you, unless you abide in Me."
John 15:4

The Lord Of The Harvest

The width, the depth, the height
The magnitude of love.
Oh Tri-une Living Majesty, oh
Holy God above.

North and South, East and West
Receive the loving flow
Revival waters moving
Will change all that we know.

The corruption of our cities
The pain of each lost soul,
Saved, healed and serving;
That's the Lord of the Harvest's goal.

Halleluia

"Do you not say, There are still four months and then comes
the harvest? Behold, I say to you, lift up your eyes and look at
the fields, for they are already white for harvest!"
John 4:35

Vessel Of Praise!

Lord, You are the Master potter
You mold and fire and sand.
Each vessel has a purpose
Designed by the Master's hand.

Lord, I have a heart-song,
Flowing through my days.
I need to ask the question,
"What is a vessel of praise?"

It would have to be very clean, Lord
Washed in Your precious Blood.
It should be filled to its brim, Lord
Full of your Holy Word.

Then the praise will keep pouring
In word, and action, and song.
Sweet fragrance will rise from the vessel,
Praising God all the day long!

Oh Lord, make me a vessel filled with praise to You.

Amen

*"For we are to God the fragrance of Christ among those who
are being saved and among those who are perishing."*
2 Corinthians 2:15

Praise in Poetry

Water - Into Wine!

The Disciples stayed with Jesus,
He taught them on the way
They entered Cana of Galilee,
early on the third day.
Mary, Jesus' mother asked
if they would please attend
The marriage celebration,
Of a special friend.

Then Mary called her Son aside,
and quietly let Him know
The bridegroom's running out of wine,
it hasn't far to go.
"Mother, what is this to you?
My time is not yet here."
Mary went on anyway —
and called the servants near.

"Do as He asks," she said,
and six large urns were brought to Him
Jesus told the servants,
"Fill the pots with water, right up to the brim."

Pitchers filled, they served the master of the feast;
who to the bridegroom gasped,
"Most serve the good wine early,
but today the best is last!"

Lord, help me to understand
why this miracle was first.
You blessed the celebration,
and many quenched their thirst.
You love us now, just as You did
in that time so long past.
Could it be that like that wedding day,
You've saved the best for last?

Thank you Jesus!

John 2: 1 - 10

Christmas, All Year Long

Yes Dear Lord, that it could be Christmas all year long
Every heart filled up with hope, in every mouth a song.
That we would be rejoicing, remembering Your birth
With angels praising God above for the miracle on earth.

It's really not beyond our reach,
just faith renewed each day
A life that's filled with You, Dear Lord,
Your presence as we pray.

Oh thank You, thank You Jesus,
I dance and sing and laugh
You came a Babe, endured the cross,
shed Blood on our behalf.

The grave could never hold You,
You conquered sin and death
Now we live to praise You,
with every joy filled breath!

"Therefore by Him let us continually offer the sacrifice of praise
to God, that is, the fruit of our lips, giving thanks to His name."
Hebrews 13:15

Mary

As a woman and a mother,
I think of Mary's ride.
The miles upon a donkey,
with Joseph by her side.
How uncomfortable to sit there,
the Child full-term within.
How precious was her burden,
God's plan to conquer sin.
With courage and with mighty faith,
she made her weary way
To pay their tax, to bear her Child,
in Bethlehem that day.

Mary paid a great price,
submitting to God's redemption plan,
The Child would live, the Man would die,
to ransom fallen man.
Now we rejoice and celebrate with
thanks unto our Lord,
Though He did die, He did arise,
He's seated next to God!
Thank You Jesus!

And Mary said:
"My soul magnifies the Lord,
And my spirit has rejoiced in God my Savior.
For He has regarded the lowly state of His maidservant;
For behold, henceforth all generations will call me blessed.
For He who is mighty has done great things for me,
And Holy is His name."

Excerpt from Mary's song.
Luke 1:46-49

The Christ Child

The Angel Gabriel, shiny and bright
came to see Mary, one lonely night.
"You'll have a Baby, Jesus by name,
Son of the Highest, forever He'll reign."

"But Sir, I'm a virgin," Mary then cried.
"All will be well," the Angel replied,
"The Holy Ghost will breathe new life into you,
fully God, fully man, faithful and true."

Mary told Joseph, for they were to be wed,
Joseph was upset by what she said.
The Angel appeared to Joseph that night,
"The Baby's from God, everything is all right."

Mary and Joseph were then quickly wed,
so Jesus would have a Mommy and Dad.
The Baby grew bigger, and one day very soon
they went to Bethlehem, where He would be born.

Mary wrapped her Babe, and held Him to her breast,
soft in her arms, her Baby she blessed.
A lovely star shone down from above,
and Angels sang a chorus of love.

Mary and Joseph were truly amazed,
as Wise Men had followed the star God had raised.
The star had led them for many long miles
to welcome a King, who came as a Child.

"Amen. Even so, come, Lord Jesus!"
Revelation 22:20b

The Gift Of Tongues

In my spirit, I soar like an eagle
Then ride on the currents of air.
With joyful anticipation,
I flow in spiritual prayer.

Sometimes it's spiritual singing
An unknown melody.
Sometimes it's spiritual warfare
Designed to set man free.

Sometimes it's spiritual labor,
The urgent travail of birth.
But always it's God's Holy Spirit,
The Comforter present on earth.

Oh God I lift up thanksgiving
For the gift of the unknown tongue.
You pray through the yielded vessel
And on earth Your will is done!

Thank You Jesus

Harvest Of Souls

If this is the last day
If this is the end
Are you ready for heaven?
Is Jesus your friend?

If you are not sure
Just where you will be,
There's a way God provided
For you and for me.

May I introduce you
To the Giver of Light?
His true Name is Jesus
He guides through the night.

Just call on His Name
He's awaiting your call
Ask Him into your life
To be Lord of all.

Ask Him for mercy
He died for your sin
Receive His forgiveness
And then enter in…

To an intimate grace
A love without measure
God's peace and God's presence,
You are His special treasure.

Amen

"For all have sinned and fall short of the glory of God,
being justified freely by His grace through the
redemption that is in Christ Jesus!"
Romans 3:23 & 24

Loving

Jesus, I love You
You please my heart so
You're my light and my peace, Lord
Wherever I go.

I lift up my eyes
My arms and my life
Your Presence is healing.
In You there's no strife.

Oh Jesus, so loving
So gracious and true
I lay down my heart, Lord
And give it to You.

Praise You my love!

Trust in the Lord with all your heart,
And lean not on your own understanding;
In all your ways acknowledge Him,
And He shall direct your paths.
Proverbs 3: 5&6

Religion Without Relationship

The Pharisees were stiff-necked,
in law they took great pride.

They tried to bait our Savior,
who graciously replied.

"If you understood the Scripture,
you would know very well,

a tender heart is valued
more than empty ritual."

Then Lord, You quietly entered
into the Church as planned,

a man attended also
with a badly crippled hand.

BR

The leaders stood to mock You,
this question You were asked,

"Is it within the law to heal,
though the Sabbath is not passed?"

Lord, You responded; "Is there one of you,
whose lamb fell in a pit,

who even on a Sabbath Day,
would not reach down to rescue it?

Surely even under this
religious law you keep,

We can be as kind to man
as we are to sheep!"

Thank you Lord, for Your mercy!

Matthew 12: 9-14

Christ Jesus, You Still Walk On Water!

The dark of evening fell quickly that night,
the Disciples went down to the sea
They entered a ship, to Capernaum bound;
and wondered, where could Jesus be?

The wind rose up strong, their ship was tossed
on the crest of the high rising tide.
Hearts quaking with fear, not believing their eyes,
They watched Jesus walk up alongside.

With love You assured them, just as You do us,
"Fear not dear friends, it is I."
Joy replaced fear, they received You aboard,
the wind went down with a sigh.

God's peace and God's presence
were with them once more,
As their ship floated silently
up to the shore!

Oh Lord, their journey is so like my life,
the night closing in all around
I knew about You, I entered the ship,
and rowed till my weak arms hung down.

Fear overcame me, I gazed at life's storms,
like a deer caught in a bright light.
Then I gave up, at the end of my strength,
and saw You walk up in the night.

Joy replaced fear, I welcomed You in
and gave You charge over my fate,
God's peace and God's presence are with me to stay,
they guide me to Heaven's fair gate.

Thank You Jesus!

"Now when evening came, His disciples went down to the sea, got into the boat, and went over the sea toward Capernaum. And it was already dark, and Jesus had not come to them. Then the sea arose because a great wind was blowing. So when they had rowed about three or four miles.
They saw Jesus walking on the sea and drawing near the boat; and they were afraid. But He said to them, 'It is I; do not be afraid.'"

John 6: 16-20

For He who is mighty has done

great things for me.

The Paraplegic Man
- Healed

The news of many miracles spread out from town to town,
Wherever Jesus went the crowds were gathered round.
Lord, You went to the wilderness, just for time to pray
the power rested on You to heal the sick each day.

The Pharisees and lawyers came from Galilee,
Judaea and Jerusalem, the miracles to see.
The streets were full of people crowding close to You,
it really was impossible to get a stretcher through.

Some men had brought their friend, a paraplegic man,
to get him to the Healer, they devised a plan.
"We'll climb the roof, remove a tile, the ropes we will secure,
we'll lower down the stretcher, friend you will be cured."

Jesus saw the faith, the boldness of their plea,
"Friend," He said, " Thy sins are forgiven thee."
The Pharisees and lawyers began to build their case,
"God alone forgives, we've a blasphemer in this place."

Jesus saw them gossiping, He could read their thoughts
He asked of them, "What reason ye, deep within your hearts,
is it easier to say, Thy sins be forgiven thee or,
rise thee up - and walk?"

"So you will know, I am the Son of Man on earth,
I'm authorized to do, either one or both."
Then to the paraplegic man, Jesus again spoke,
"Arise, take up your bed, and go."

Immediately the man rose up, and lifted up his bed,
Glorifying God, and praising, he did as Jesus said.
The crowd amazed, was filled with fear and awe,
they rubbed their eyes, incredulous, giving glory unto God!

Amen

Luke 5: 16 -26

To God be the Glory!

Prodigal! Come Home

The Father walked in blessing, he had two beloved sons
But the younger was ungrateful of all his Dad had done.

He demanded his inheritance; far ahead of time
The Father gave his portion, each and every dime.

The son then gathered all, and journeyed far away
He squandered his inheritance on self- indulgent play.

His wealth soon gone, then famine struck
and he experienced need
He was hired by a farmer,
a herd of pigs to feed.

Hunger raged within him,
if he had found a way
He'd have eaten of the pig slop;
pride no longer seemed to pay.

Then he came back to sanity and realized what he'd lost
His rebelliousness was ended; he began to count the cost.

" In my Father's house the servants
have bread enough to spare
Maybe he will hire me,
I'll be a servant there."

Confession formed within his heart,
"Oh Father I have sinned,
Against heaven and against you,
I'm unworthy to come in."

His Father saw him coming,
compassion rose up strong
He held and kissed and loved him,
as the son confessed his wrong.

The Father called then for a ring,
a robe and sandals for his feet
The finest fatted calf was killed
and cooked for them to eat.

"For this my son was dead, but now he is alive
Was lost but now is found, thank God he did survive."

Oh Father God, You love us, and when we turn from sin
Your loving arms enfold us and welcome us back in!

Amen

Luke 15: 11 -24

Thanking God for Family

Into the home of my birth
Our God deposited seed
A seed of spiritual hunger
That only God can feed.

From roots of family and farming
Roots deep in God's fertile land
We'll rise up in love for Jesus
As my people come forth to stand.

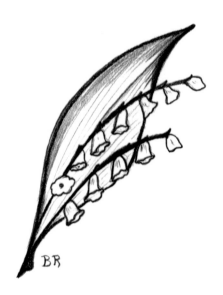

We'll stand in the Lordship of Jesus
We'll finally take up our cross
We'll march in God's End-time Army
As harvesters reaching the lost!

We laid on the altar our grief
The loss of a son so young.
In God's time we'll join him in heaven
Glad that our life's race is run.

For now the cursing is over
It's canceled in Jesus great Name.
We receive generational blessing
We'll never be the same.

Amen

Thank you Jesus!

"May the Lord give you increase more and more,
You and your children.
May you be blessed by the Lord,
Who made heaven and earth."
Psalm 115: 14&15

Resurrection Sunday

The lovely white lily,
The sunrise, the Cross
The mourning is over
The grief and the loss.

We're standing before
An empty tomb!
With Angels around us
Dispelling the gloom.

This Sunday morning
Outshines all the rest.
Our God is alive!
This news is the best.

Thank You Jesus

BR

First Love

I refocus my heart, Lord
Fully on You.
I repent of my sin
The wrong things that I do.
Rekindle my spirit
With fire from above
I'll worship with passion,
In my first-love.

I submit my mind, Lord
My will must now bow.
My agenda is Yours, Lord.
Please teach me how
To worship You fully
To walk in Your Way
To serve with obedience,
In You, Jesus, I'll stay.

Amen

"Nevertheless I have this against you,
that you left your first love.
Remember therefore from where you have fallen;
repent and do the first works, or else I will remove
your lampstand from it's place — unless you repent."
Revelation 2: 4 & 5

Our Little Ones

"There is a comfy, cozy place, a place to snuggle down
I'm hugged, kissed and cuddled, then my blankets
wrapped around.

Each night they come to tuck me in,
and hear me when I pray
I settle in a peaceful sleep; then wake to a bright new day!"

Oh God, that all the little ones would be in loving care,
With parents who would love them,
and cover them with prayer.

But in this fallen world of ours, things have gone so wrong,
That many precious little ones are weak instead of strong.

The family is in trouble, the enemy is wild
The attack is on our people, centered on each child.

It begins with each conception, the abortion clinics' plan,
To kill as many innocents, as it possibly can.

Add to this the birthing's that our young mothers face,
With medical complications, only rescued by Your grace.

Oh Lord, I bow before You, repentant of our sin,
Please cleanse this land of wickedness; Holy Spirit enter in.

The blood of unborn babies cries out from our soil,
Our people serve the bankers, bound to debt and toil.

There is just one solution, You paid it on the Cross
May we have courage to repent – soon, before we're lost.

To stand in intercession, for Holy Spirit fire,
To burn the filthy dross from us, oh may I never tire!

Dear Lord, I have a vision of people loving You,
Of us loving each other as You asked us to do.

Jesus, You have loved us more then we can tell,
That love was proved on Calvary, on a Cross in Israel.

God to You be the Glory!

Amen

"Restore us, O God of our salvation,
And cause Your anger toward us to cease.
Will You be angry with us forever?
Will you prolong your anger to all generations?
Will you revive us again,
That Your people may rejoice in you?
Show us Your mercy, Lord,
And grant us Your salvation."
Psalm 85: 4-7

In His Presence!

"My child:

You have asked the question, 'What would Jesus do?'

*I came to heal the brokenhearted,
and that, My love, was you.*

*You've called to Me and worshipped Me,
you have sought My face,*

*You've entered in My very heart,
you're covered with My grace!*

*Please understand, I've sown in you,
a very special seed-*

*Through Me you'll touch the broken hearts,
of those who are in need.*

I've given you authority to loose the devils' schemes,

*To bring them out, and set them free,
so they'll fulfill My dreams!*

I call you now to leave the world,
the flesh and self behind,

I'll cover you, provide for you,
the cares will leave your mind.

I long to fellowship with you,
a special time apart-

My Word will be alive in you,
a planting in your heart.

I have supplied your healing,
I've spoke it; it is done,

You must appropriate it,
walk upright as a son.

My precious Blood was shed for you;
you're covered by its' power,

My anointing is upon you,
this is your finest hour!"

Thank you Jesus!

Our Blood Washed Family!

Oh Jesus I thank You
For the Blood that You shed
Pour over this family
Cover us... red!

Wash us so clean, Lord
Make us brand new
Washed white as snow, Lord
Covered in You.

Your presence is joy, Lord
And in joy is strength
Your love is an ocean
Great width, depth and length.

Oh Lord, for this family
Your purpose will stand
Fill us Holy Spirit
We'll harvest this Land.

Amen

"Come now let us reason together,
Says the Lord,
Though your sins are like scarlet,
They shall be as white as snow;
Though they are red like crimson,
They shall be as wool."
Isaiah 1:18

The Woman at the Well

*First published as foreword to the book
"Out of Self... let go and let God!"
by Sharon Ouwerkerk.*

The Pharisees were quarreling,
Lord, as people often do.
Dissenting words to come between
Your precious friend so true,
Who baptized more? Who drew more in ?
John the Baptizer, or You?

The way was long from Judaea,
en route to Galilee,
You walked all night on weary feet,
the wind blew from the sea.
You traveled through Samaria,
Sychar the town to gain
A place to rest and be refreshed,
the well on Jacob's plain.

Dear Lord, You rested by the well,
the shade a welcome place.
A woman came, with bucket tied,
the years upon her face.
You asked for drink, she questioned You,
A Jewish man, she knew-
Would never ask a thing of her,
but still Your drink she drew.

You spoke of "Living Water" Lord,
a gift to her and me.
And though she didn't understand,
she asked and she received.
You asked about her husband then,
she answered, she had none.
Though past were five,
and even now was living with a man.

Oh grant me Lord, a humble heart
that I will answer true,
Of broken past relationships,
of sin that I've walked through.
When she spoke truth,
You opened up her understanding Lord.
She recognized the Prophet then,
and listened to the Word.

"Oh Woman, I say believe,
for now the time is here,
The place you worship does not count,
be it far or near.
You worship now you know not what,
but I tell you true
You'll worship soon, the Living God,
Salvation's of the Jew."

You taught her then to worship God,
in Spirit and in truth.
I've sought You, Lord, and now today,
that's how I worship You.
Oh Lord, You look into the heart...
I pray that I may be
A woman stripped of pride and greed,
able to believe.

The woman left her jug behind,
and went to tell the news
That all might come and then receive
the "Living Water" too.
The Word of God, is reaching out
to whomsoever will-
Let go of self and look to God,
His mission to fulfill.

The days go by so quickly now –
my life is running out
Help me to seek Your face, dear Lord,
without a shred of doubt!

John 4:1 - 26

To God be the Glory!

Calling The Lost!

You know about God, the heaven's declare!
His magnificent glory is evident there.
You know about Jesus, you knew as a child
But as you grew older, you became wild.

You worked very hard to better yourself,
Even tried lotteries, hoping for wealth.
The Word of the Lord, you frequently heard,
But your heart was hard, you resisted God's Word.

Now you are aging, your family is grown,
Your idols are polished, your life work is sown.
You're spiritually bankrupt, and facing your end,
And Jesus still loves you, He still is your friend.

He died on the Cross, for you and for me,
He shed His life Blood on Calvary's tree.
Then He arose and is seated at the right hand of God,
He'll come into your heart, just give Him your word.

Believe in your heart, and speak the words out,
Repenting of sin will turn your life about.
God's Word clearly tells us; and God's Word is true,
Eternal salvation is waiting for you.

"For God so loved the world that He gave His only begotten Son,
that whosoever believes in Him should not perish but have
everlasting life."

John 3:16

Praise in Poetry   107

Jesus, My Beloved

You showed me the best love I could possibly see
Before I even knew You, You gave Your life for me.

Oh Jesus, I'm thankful, I owe You everything
I give myself to You, my Eternal King!

The love You have for me, You have for everyone,
Your Blood paid our debt Lord, Calvary's work is done.

Oh Jesus, I love You, I owe You everything
All I am is Yours; Lord, my Eternal King!

Oh thank you, dearest Savior, Holy Living Lord
You are the Way, the Truth, the Life as spoken in Your Word.

Precious Lord, I love You, I owe You everything
My life I give to You Lord, my Eternal King!

Oh take me, mold me, use me; the harvest field is white
With praises, prayer and fasting, help me reap till the night.

Oh Jesus, how I love You, You are my everything
You are worthy, precious Savior... our Eternal King!

"Let my mouth be filled with Your praise
And with Your glory all the day."
Psalm 71:8

Living In Jesus

Sweet Jesus I remember
The ways You've blessed me so,
Our great salvation benefits
That make my spirit grow.

Household salvation, I have prayed for
The Foundation Stone is in place,
This family has received You
Now please help us to seek Your face.

May we grow to serve You, Lord
In a unique and special way,
That we will show the world Your love
At home, at work, at play!

Thank You Jesus!

"Believe on the Lord Jesus Christ, and you
will be saved, you and your household."
Acts 16:31

Praise and glory and honor to You, Jesus
Mighty God, and Prince of Peace.

The Leper

I think of the leper walking in death,

Despised by all, including himself.

His flesh was diseased, corrupted by sin

He was visible evidence of the fall of man.

But inside that man the spirit was soft,

Open to hear the good news of God.

He lifted his eyes from his earthly plight,

And fell down to worship the Giver of light.

Jesus reached forth His hand, healing was there,

The man received answer to his faith- filled prayer.

The leprous condition of that humble man

Is the state of us all without salvation's plan.

Thank You Jesus!

"When He was come down from the mountain, great multitudes followed Him. And behold, a leper came and worshipped Him, saying, 'Lord, if You are willing, You can make me clean.' Then Jesus put out His hand and touched him, saying, 'I am willing; be cleansed.' Immediately his leprosy was cleansed."
Matthew 8: 1-3

Halleluia!

Holiness

Daniel purposed in his heart,
he made a stand within
That he would not defile himself,
that he'd be free of sin.
For Daniel was a Jewish youth,
he knew the Jewish law
The foods and drink that were allowed,
as Moses heard from God.

Each one of us who has been taught
to walk God's Holy Way,
Must purpose in our own heart that
a standard we must raise.
To fulfill God's call upon our lives,
and live as He has shown
Through the shed Blood of God's own Son,
we will not walk alone.

Praise be to You, Jesus!

"But Daniel purposed in his heart that he would not defile
himself with the portion of the king's meat, nor with the wine
which he drank: therefore he requested of the prince of the
eunuchs that he might not defile himself."

Daniel 1:8

Praise in Poetry